Words of steel and velvet

poems and texts by Danielle Baraka

To S, L&M and my parents for being who they are.

Special and warm thanks to Federica for her help and support.

D.

Table of contents

I ~Transition

II ~ An Irish journey

I - Transition

Linda: "Nobody's perfect. There was never a perfect person around. You just have half-angel and half-devil in you" ~ 'Days of Heaven' (Terence Malick - 1978)

Transition

Mourning my father
Mourning my mother
Mourning my husband
Mourning my lover
Mourning my fingers
Through his hair

Mourning
The touch
The laughter
the cry
Of the elevating
Momentum

Mourning
The Lands
I'll never see

The cut out
Ripped
Insomniac
Dreams

Two Diamonds
Of fragile
Blossoming
Enlightening
A belly
Of desperate
Striving
Freedom

Breathing

My painful
Insightful

Rebirth

Clockwise

I have seen

Their childhood
Fly away

Like an impatient bird

Hastened
By an hurried clock

Beating too fast

Leaving
The magic
To a past

That yet
Looks like
Present

The run
Toward
An early flight

Traitor
Time

Insidiously

Had caught us

Elsewhere

So busy
With this crazy Fight
Struggling so hard

Still
The vital
Reciprocal
Necessity

Of A kiss

On the forehead

A sweet hug
To comfort

Some Funny words
To take a breath

To feel alive

And see a smile

Of Revival

A signal
Of rebirth

Out of the Dark

A lullaby
To calm down

The fears
The invincible
Blood

Flowing
Across the miles
Beyond Silence
Powerful
And Serene

From them to me
From me to them

Misty mind

Here
I die again
And from these thousand deaths
The bitter taste
Poisonously
Toxic
Upon the tongue

Trembling deaths
Of dislocation

Unbalanced
Breath

Dismantled
Passion

So familiar

These lost
And lonely falls

These dawns
Rising toward
This perpetual
Human quest

Red roses

Red roses laid

Upon a bed of thorns

Tired dreams

Nipped in the bud

Bloody hell screams

cutting off respectfulness

In the white moonlight

Stifled by the hands of a meaningless fate

Words

Baffled,

Unheard,

Mutilated

Reduced to nothingness

Heavy silence

And time for sacrifice

The moon is high

The beast under transformation
can't fight the demon's grasp
Fulfilled by the pure white shape
of an idealized glint
Soft shadows
Splashing in blindness
Warm kiss on lips of bliss
Lightening an etheral fire
Peeping through the sinful door
Opened to what may be
An insolent truth.

A kiss

Shivering
Thundering
and bright
Tearing off
A fragile impulse
Lingering
On the edge of a dream

Cloudy, misty
And proud
In its disobedience

The unsaid
The invisible one
Kept warm and soft
Stronger than a wave
Of Desire

The secret in your mouth
Revealed
by unconcealed lips
A desperate bliss
of dew
Rolling upon
My lips

Forbidden, hidden, stolen

Maybe
There'll be no rest

The soft and strong scent
Of an orchid

The taste
Of a timeless bliss

"How did it happen that their lips come together?□ How does it happen that birds sing, that snow melts, that the rose unfolds, that the dawn whitens behind the stark shapes of trees on the quivering summit of the hill? A kiss, and all was said." ~ Victor Hugo

His name

His name

Twirling in my head
Like million poppies
Blossoming in my breast
Like water lilies
Caressing my belly
Like sweet daisies

His name

Letters
Gathered
In signification
Hanging upon
My silent
Mouth

Rapture

The traitor snake
Had crawled
And shut his eyes
And won that final fight
And so he laid his burden down
And rested in her arms
Now mourning hands can't grasp
The breath of life
That death has robbed away
Wrapped up in iron coldness
Confined in inner end

It would

I would have to say nothing
Breathing the perfect feeling
The perfect time
The perfect view
The perfect angle
On a perfect nape of the neck
Studiously bent over its work
Cherished by a perfect light
In a perfect silent day
Time standing still
With the delicacy of a masterpiece beauty
Summer sunshine on the skin
Celebrating the curves, the wrinkles and the soft details
Of the worshiped one..

Into the wild

I wished I had a cliff to climb,
A sea-shore to walk through,
A wild land to cross over
In a breathless reinvigorating race,
Going ahead,
I realized that time had no anchor and that I had no age
That we are thrown into this world
Like free electrons swept by wind
That have to make their way
Sometimes filled with wonder
Sometimes filled with pain
All my wanderings led me there
Into your wild landscape
In a so unconventional, unwanted way...

I will

I will create
Expose, deliver and offer
Give away
Model, undo, and build again
I will fight
With your breath by my side
Knowing that I can't reach
Or embrace you
I will feel the world
I will decode, translate
Build up bridges between islands
Between signs,
Between your words and mine
I will write
The most sensuous words
To tell your absent touch
To tell the most precious feeling
Bringing out the brightest sparks
Letting out the butterfly
Freed from my white shoulder
I will tell
The thrill
The dizzy rise
The lightness in the breast
The priceless quest
In this place of no name,
Among the multitude

Summer whispers

The lightness of the dragonfly
Grasped my wandering gaze
I took a chance
To catch
This furtive green fairy
In the hollow of my hands
The twirling of its flight
Unites with the sacred
Unreachable music
Of this static summer day
Bewildered,
By the window pane
I let a dream escape
Out of the unlocked prison
Of my thoughts
A liberated weight
A murmur hanging on the lips
The stream
Of some wondering words
A breath, a sigh,
Floating in heavy silence
Dancing softly
Like an insect wing
Lifted by the warm, shiny season

I dream waves of you

Guess who I am
Beneath the surface
Of my dreams
Under the mist
Of my silent
Image
Understanding
Beyond the outlines
Behind the shadow
Of my hat
Without a word
Leaving my mouth

Like twin-brothers
Mirror
Of well-being and warmth
Alike and different
Among the crowd

Waiting
Settled like an habit
An unexpected grasp
Of passion
Leading to nowhere

There
A voice is needed
In the impatience
Of the moment
A breath, a sigh,
A cry of joy

Guilty
In its accomplishment
Lips,
Sex,
Neck,
Body and flesh
Smile,
Silence
What is love?
A word,
A laughter,
A touch
Of the mind
A cosmic union

The soul
In redemption

Partners

And the will
To cradle and calm
The turmoils
And the pains

Feeling
Caressing
A soul
I kiss
The devastated field
Of a wandering heart

Listening

I understand
Saying no word
No need...

Desire

I look and love
A perfect neck,
a perfect shoulder
A perfect tone

Warm and soft
Wrinkles and marks
Of lovable truth
Sparkling shadows
Of unreachable
Pleasure
Eyes and hands
Sublimated and worshiped

A stolen gift

Infiltrating
Softly

Under the
Thick reality

You
Reading between the lines
Of my damned thoughts
Killing doubts
Real wounds

Sticking to the skin
And leaving scars

Telling with your words
Of steel and velvet
The world

Your world

Your words
Of transcendental thinking

Raising

Sharing

Where innocence and sin
Do unite in despair
Making us

Feel

Alive

Dull lullaby

The fear

Of the night to come

Hanging on white sheets
The only calming down gesture
In this primal anxiety

Shadows
Dancing in the night
Threatening
As I try to retain
The beauty of a rose
In my confused mind
The fountain
With the birds nearby
In the broad daylight
I try to unfold the ritual
Of a familiar song
A sweet lullaby of comfort
That could chase the shadows away

But the candle goes out quickly
The melody becomes a murmur
A sigh
Vanishing in the darkness
Of a fast beating heart

The fight seems like
The ultimate one
A fight of no return..

Until tomorrow night...
Cold sweat

I hang on to
The saving thin white light
Under the bedroom door
The smothered voices of adults
In the room nearby
The changing intonations
Of the TV program

Confined there,
I understand,
Become aware
Of
Death
Merciless, irreversible
The wave,
That will take us away

Late, in the silent night
Where thoughts learn how to grow
Familiar echoes
Reverberate
As I still cannot sleep
In the tired
Uncalmed
Adult body clay

Too late

Too late to meet in the garden
Too late to share the dance
The dizzy grace
Of an enchanted dawn
His hands
Building up
Sleepy palaces
Cultivating
Magnificent sterile gardens
Silent
Powerful master of the place
Inviolable fortresses
Among stones
Of magnificent coldness
Alone,
In bare armor,
I am the warrior
cut by the icy wind
of an uncompromising winter
Walking toward
The warmth of a smiling sun
Colored bright desires
Hurt in their unhappy corolla
The heart
In a thundering bang
Feeling the lost of a passion
Of a treacherous failure
Entanglements
Of suffocating resignation
In the devastated field
Of irreversible disunion

Thoughts

Anchor was cast on the shore
Of an unforeseen absence

A voice
A body
Absent

In an absurd way

Absolute
Absence

Like an empty jar
Of desolation
Shaking the night

Absence

Resounding
In an endless echoe
Filling the veins
With an obsessive poison

Body left
Immaculate and offended
Desired and unwanted
Loved
By a delicious
Absent touch

Only words
To tell the joy

Words
To tell the turmoil
Words
Like a treasure
Lovely kept in one's deep self
Fusion
Of desire mixed
With irrevocable duties
Keeping passion away

Bleeding wounds
Of clear-sighted conscious innocent
Devotion

Eyes
Containing the infinite song
Of unfolding destinies
Unmastered tragedies
Our human particles
Scattered, gathered and melt
Thrown in the stellar space
Compacted
As one
In flesh and mind
Breath
Measured and tamed
Compelled by forbidden echoes

Lovers, brothers,
Drifted away

Dreamers
Both blinded and fulfilled
By the mysterious beauty

Of this imperfect sacred world

Children
Wondering
And brought back
To the essential feeling of life

Rebirth

Hurt like Hell
Fallen down
On a tired ground
In the monastic, silent
Familiar antechamber
Of the mind

The Sacred
Guessed
Beyond absurd shadows
To which
A sense
Must be given

Life's bewilderment

The dream
That was dreamt
Caught in a frame
Mistaken
Where all was wrong

Blindness

Dragging
A whole wagon
Of inner
Damnation

Aspiring to
Higher
Transcending

Fulfillment

A faithful
Engagement

Implied
In the dizzy
Twirling ballet

Falling down...

To be born again

Breathing

Time
Got lost
In a breath

Your breath
Your laugh
Unthinkable
Extinguished
Candle

Sacred words

Fatherly said

Looks and silences

Strangling doubts
In loneliness
And words
Unsaid

Passionate
Vital
Impulses
Your Passions
From your veins
To mine
I
Got lost
When your breath
Faded
In emptiness

Reflections

Was it
A second birth?
Born
Out of a corrupted sight
Merging
Blinding
In boldness
And evidence

Sweet, soft, sliding
Colorful sins
Guilty, doubtful
And proud
In innocence
Finding their place

Like a long-time
Scattered puzzle

Blurred visions
Of a mistaken mind

Which truth?
Which wisdom?
Which pains?

Self-will
Choosing to choose
My freedom
And my chains

Worshiped

Forbidden
Sublimated
Skin and soul

Surrendering in mastering

Until the smooth
And powerful vision
Of a soul
Liberated from
The shadows on the wall

Words

Craze for words
Desire to write again
Greedy necessity
Powerful
Concentrated
And fluid flow
The kind of
Magical
Alchemy
Apparently
Mastered
Carefully chosen
Words
But
Immediatly
Dispossessed of them
As soon as
On the white sheet
A life of their own
Seeds
Scattered
In the barren air
Belonging to
An unknown
Destination

Illusion

There
I stand

There
I guess

The invisible
The unsaid

The passionate
Passion

The overpowering
'invention'

The almighty
Pleasurable
Illusion

Moment of eternity

From Here to There
From There to Here

The Nowhere place

The Everywhere place

Overpowering
All the horizons

Transcending
All the logics
Of Time

I meet him
There

In sinful
Feverish thoughts
Of illusion

A whirling of warmth

A hot red lip of foolishness

A white heart of hope

Red and bound
Embraces
Sensuous
Detachments

Skin, sweat, blood
Fears and delights

Burning

The Secret point
The Sacred print
On the fascinated mind

The delight of the
Forbidden bliss

The urging necessity
The sublimated beauty
The everlasting madness

The most
Pleasurable
Unreachable
Heaven

Submission bound
To the desire

Waiting for
The uncertain
Reward

Getting close
To the feeling
The almost perfect
Sensation

Powerfully present
And yet
So far
Constantly
On the run

Like the snapshot of an instant
Suspended in time
Freed and escaped
From the immutable constraint
Of the frame

Seeing

The mind
In such a wise
Disposition

The eye
As a witness

The will
To embrace
To live
To laugh
To deliver delight
To keep silence

The love
Of simple things
That overflow the heart

Acceptance

Not a resignation
But an encounter
With the world's
sap and essence

Understanding

Human nature

In its predictable
Unpredictability

An endless inspiration

I don't know
Where
I'm running to

No road

Leading
To you

No close-up
No closeness
And yet

Each particle
Of this amazing world
Seems filled with
The rapturous
Sensation
Of You

Strangely
I find you
Where
I find me too

No togetherness
No rest

But a wild
Mindblowing
Electric dream

Launched on the rails

A breathless quest

Upon the hills

Among the towns

Into the dark
Heavenly places
of our minds

Wild freedom

Extracted from
The howling depths
Of a merciless
Desire

Body and Soul
Restless

Carried by
The dream

Of a kiss

Upon

This perfect neck

The sticky side of the adhesive tape

A question

Caressing, inviting...and close..

Parallelism

The quest
Of two foreign souls

Searching for an escape
In immobility

They will tell
In some improbable spaces

The print
And the echoes
On the mind

The stirless journey

The promise of a merciless gift

The poisonous passion

Interlaced by a thousand doubts

A dream of lightness

Trapped in a mouth
Full of golden dust

A bruised skin
A misty soul

A story to be written

The amazing game of surrender
To the idleness of no decision

To see or not to see
To say or not to say

See & Say
The re-shaped world

Entangled in the echoes
Of a banging collusion

Discovering, sharing, learning...

They knew

Dominance
Shared and equal

A merciless balance of powers

Clenched teeth
Of a voluptuous fight
Whispers, cries and silences...

Left on the sticky side
Of the adhesive tape...

A journey

To celebrate
The unsaid
The unvisible

The Duality

That sounds yet
Like an evidence

Half-sleep
Powerful dreams
Wrapped into
A coat of wind
Into a flame
Of possession
Opening the eyes
With this salty taste
On the lips

The eternal bliss
Of a suspended Time
The arms
Wrapped around
Perfect shoulders

Kissing a ghostly neck..
An echoe
In the sound box
Of a wild
Beating heart

Telling
The red dark
Spitting lava
Grazing, disturbing
and yet
Or so
Pushing the will
Forward

Among the dizzy
Soft, guilty scents

Among the world's simple
Complex multiplicity

Between The abundance
And the first, original
Illusional emptiness

Freedom

On the tip of
A blade of grass
Over the clouds
Over the hills
Among the mad crowded places
In the silence
Of the darkest caves

Travelling
Wandering souls
Of tireless dreamers

Perpetually
Re-building
The dismantled dream

Like a never ending
Symphony

An embroidery
To be perfected

Inexhaustibly

The magic
Crossing the mind

And in the end
The unfolded
The unexpected
The sublime
Logical, evident
Perfect fitting

Perceived
But not reached yet

Resting
On the wet shores
Of an untamed
Ocean's
Merciless
Music

Thoughts on a New Year's day

Man's hand
Pointing

Man's mind
Counting

Clock on
Clock in

Big Wave

Carrying
Dreams
Along

Moving
Twisted
Ribbon

With no beginning
And no end

Printed with
Unutterable

Scars
And Pleasures

Some to remember

Some to forget

Thoughts on a winter's day

A vision

Extended to the fringe
Of the horizon
In an endless echo

Responding to
Questions
Without an answer

Desires
without an harbour

Sensations
Both dark and enlightened

The powerful union
Sinuous
Sensitive
In shivering
Desires and fears

Body
Held tight
In a sense
Of vulnerability and trust

The mind
Sublimated
And transcended

Waves upon waves

Questions upon questions

The mysterious

Impalpable

Alchemy

Desire

Storm-like
Invading and proud
A burning breath
A light capsizing shiver
An awakening
A struggle
To reach
The unattainable
To bring together
The pieces
Of a scattered dream

A feverish dew
Upon red burning lips

Some words
Provocative and bold
Blossoming
With dark echos
On the subjugated mind

Breath contained

Each square meter of the skin
Being mobilized
Flaring oul
With desire

In an endless
stirring
Blossoming quest

Printings on the whiteness

The clock
Suspended at a breath
A concentration
Of body and mind
Immobilized
Almost frozen
Into their own
Reflection
That not even
The barking of the dog
Disturbs

The 'reverie'
The wondering
The fight

Stained
With the unconfortable
Taste
Of hesitation

Pleasurable
Burning
Bitterness

Touching
The eager wet lips
For a questioned desire

Dreams, Hopes
Glorified
And yet
Put in the balance
By the deeply anchored
Servile Morality

Habits
Like a too much sticking
Second skin

The will
Of the old soul
Transfigured into
Stimulating pageantries

The merciless
Attraction
Of the other self

Ashes of Angels
Compromised
By a powerful
Black leather echo

The ambivalent
Wild thoughts

Travelling insomnias
When the devils infiltrate
Into the sacrilegious night
Dark temptations
Of anchored certainties

Duality
In the immense motionless
Loneliness

Not a resignation
But a Purpose
A long process
A quest
Where the Sacred and the secular meet
In an almost Religious ecstatic feeling

Suspended in Time
And 'moved' by Time

An evidence
The mind knows
And that the body
knows too

The weight

The price to pay
The amount of the sacrifice
The Choice to make
The freedom
To express

Black blood
Flowing out of the pen
Into the veins
Of the Sacred sheet

Dark thoughts
Spread among
The white
Immaculate
Winter snow

Outside the frame

A will
A twisted thought
A dream
Another view
Another angle
A flight
Out of the frame

Deeply rooted
Into the wild belly

A loneliness
An habit
A quest

Imperturbable
And free
Not in the rank
Never

Always endangered
By the inner, fatal
Stubbornness

The faithfulness
To stoical

Insubordination

The Diamante poems

Infinity,
Dizzy, mysterious, cosmic
Puzzles, dazzles, questions
Time, space, love, soul
Splits, frees, burdens, concludes
Irrevocable, fixed, dark
Ending

Passion
Sensuous, bright, thoughtful
Burning, raising, revealing
Desire, thrill, nothingness, tears
Hurting, bleeding, cutting
Unenlighted, careless
Coldness

La
multitude
Bruyante, agitée
Mélange, tourbillone, absorbe
Le flot, l'essaim, la distance, l'exil
Etouffe, libère, questionne, écoute
La silencieuse, vide
Solitude

(Multitude
Noisy, hectic
Mixing, absorbing, twirling
Streem, swarm, distance, exile
Suffocates, frees, questions, listens to
The empty, silent,
Solitude)

Inspired by 'The Diamante poem' form:
The Diamante poem is arranged in a diamond pattern using seven lines in the following manner:

Line 1: noun (noun, the opposite of line 7)
Line 2: adjective, adjective (2 adjectives describing line 1)
Line 3: verb, verb, verb (3 verbs relating to line 1)
Line 4: noun, noun, noun (2 nouns about line 1 and 2 nouns about line 7)
Line5: verb, verb, verb (3 verbs realting to line 7)
Line 6: adjective, adjective (2 adjectives describing line 7)
Line 7: noun (noun, the opposite of line 1)

Memories of a Parisian scene

He promptly took off his long grey suit and put it on his chair. His gestures being fluid and assured.
The restaurant was very busy at this moment of the day and he openly said with a soft smile that he was really hungry now.

I smiled.Just smiled.Trying not to show too much of my excitement to be here with him alone, again...

He is eating his dish in a very refined, delicate and prompt way, with the apparent delight of someone who has had a very busy day and can finally relax...

The wine is good and soft going down the throat.
My mind, feeling dizzy...

I think this man is not common, as if something unutterably tragic was linked with him, with his story. As if he hold some kind of terrible secret.
Something dealing with Passion.

I think I love the way he talks, softly, but also with a strong determination. With clearly articulated words.

He says that what he has loved the most in this film is the 'orgies' scenes...the beauty of the naked bodies moving under the silky sheets.
I have seen the film and I know what he means.

I can feel the seduction is under way, as I try to

restrain a fast breath.

His face, his expression is usually calm but he also has a way to distill an extraordiany sense of humour and provocation, which I love.

The night is dark and cold outside, contrasting with the warmth of the agitated Parisian restaurant.

I think I'd love to stay there for hours, keeping on talking and talking, and laughing...

I can see his perfect suit, his perfect grey hair that gives him something almost British.

We go on talking.

This man holds more than some knowledge and common sense.

I am fascinated by this apparent distinction, as well as by the partly hidden, tortured pains he seems to hold inside.

I can feel a closeness, a warmth, a troubling complicity, a thrill that will follow me all the rest of my life.

I think 'Silence' must be possible with this man, too.

Perfection of a pure moment, with only a simple soft kiss in the back of the head.

Time suspended , between a book, a thought, a look, a silence.

That is the feeling he has left me...

II ~ An Irish journey

"Her lips touched his brain as they touched his lips, as though they were a vehicle of some vague speech and between them he felt an unknown and timid pleasure, darker than the swoon of sin, softer than sound or odor." ~ James Joyce

Ireland I – Killarney and the Kerry area February 2011.

A cold and sunny morning.

And out of that cold sunny morning, what could have seemed a total loneliness, blossomed into a real sense of freedom.

There...

Loneliness, there...

I'm putting down my clothes at your feet. Naked and free. To meet you through the alchemy of a mysterious equation. Timeless.

United with the deep, strong unchanging roots. A strength made of stones, leaves, lakes, flowers and mountains. Impertubably crossed by a constantly changing air.

Light clouds gathered in farandole around the unperturbed mountains.A sense of eternity..Giving to my world a new meaning. A universal transcending feeling.

Some coloured sheeps lost in the bushes, almost still. Planted like stones in the landscapes.
And the delicious sweetness of being aware of all the possible choices out of there.

I can guess the stake. Experiencing the golden price of Silence. Like a tightrope walker.

Either you fly, either you die.

I know that standing there is like a gift, all along with the will and the deep breath taken. Conscious of the inner Loneliness. Of the cardinal points, and of my own centre of gravity. *The point of balance...*

Ireland II Kerry - 22 feb 2011.

Leaving Dublin.
I'm on my way to Killarney.
Will be back in two days.

Leaving the city. Toward Kerry...Reaching the swampy fields, the wide green spaces and the mountains in the distance.
Early in the morning...So strange to be here.
Thinking about the girls who must be sleeping quietly in their bed, in France.

Reaching Killarney on a soft rainy day.'Jumping' into another world. I usually take quickly my marks in a new place. So lovely.

The atmosphere...ALL changes there.
Two hours walking in the National Park.The soft rain has stopped.

Breathing...Tasting...Living...in an almost quasi solitude.
Just crossing a few people, most of them walking their dog.

A small river and some gardens...strangely curved trees...flowers starting to blossom as the promise of an early coming Spring.

Pushing my body. Pushing my mind. 'Obliging' myself. 'Throwing' myself into this world.

(....)

The Warmth of a small coffee shop...Hot coffee and delicious cake.
I love the song on the radio, hummed by this handsome Irish man.
Reading the Irish Times. Exhausted but happy.

Feeling free.
The next mysterious moment on my fingertips...

Golden dust and dreams – Ireland III
(Belfast : 25/26 février 2011)

'I've got a ticket for the fats city..' (Katie Melua 'Belfast)

I can still feel the early busy life of the train station hall...and then, the landscapes, unexpected...
Being so far from home brings such a special state of mind..
But I know I have to be there. Like an appointment. Maybe to find answers, or not.
At least to be in the condition of being able to stand back, and to think...and to consider things under a totally new point of view.
What will I find?

The coming out of the station is like a chock, a feeling to be lost, distraught, not knowing where to start. Not knowing 'how' to start. How am I going to 'meet' the city, its 'heart', its beauties and its pains?

Relieved from the burden of my luggage, I suddenly feel as light as a bird. Almost 'gliding' and 'flying' in the streets, eager, loving, peaceful and free.
Drinking the colors, the smells, the movements of the crowd, the life...
The perfectly aligned streets. Saying so much to me. Meaning so muche to me, and the buildings of red brick walls, leaving a unique print in the mind, a feeling that belongs to 'there'.

I know I'd need more time.

First evening, at the 'Ulster Hall':

Maybe there could have been no better way to meet the city.
The magnificence of the place. The organ, throning, majestically on the stage, as if a sacred rite was imminent.
And the almost 'religious' resounding pure voice of the opera singer , lifting you higher for a moment, to a transcendental felicity.

The pubs....

....grasping you in their arms.Wrapped in the warm, musical, joyful, singing accents. The proximity of the 'whatever' possible.
The dizziness that catches you there doesn't leave you...Growing the thirst bigger. The thick, dark bitter taste on the tongue, awakening a blissfull and guilty pleasure.

But yet, the freshness of a new day carries you out again, elsewhere. Still wandering. Still wondering..
Questionning the silent walls, the ghostly mountains in the distance, the faces that I cross...
The 26th is my birthday, here, in Belfast.
Strange...and, strangely (and abnormally?) happy with my loneliness.

The mind, elevated.
The body, freed.

And not wanting to let this feeling go.

These...
Golden dust and dreams.

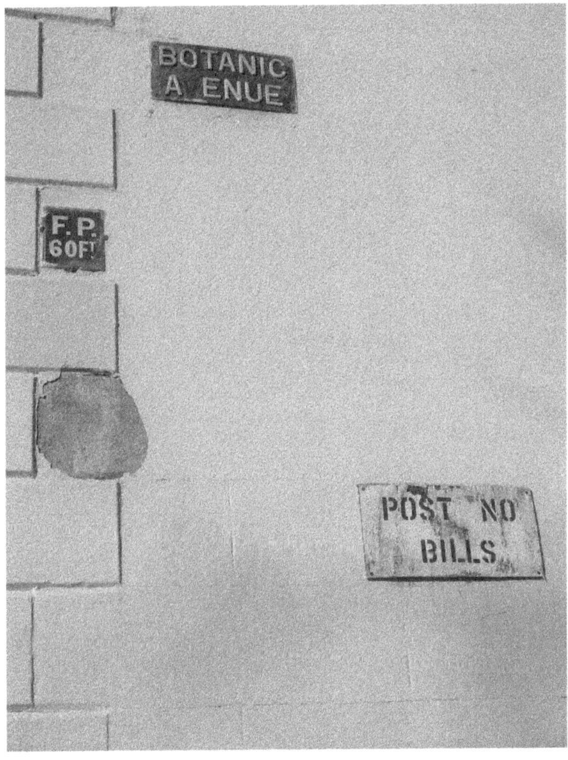

www.ingramcontent.com/pod-product-compliance
Ingram Content Group UK Ltd.
Pitfield, Milton Keynes, MK11 3LW, UK
UKHW020234250726
13967UKWH00001B/366

9 781471 611971